The Words of Jesus

"Remember the words of the Lord Jesus, how He said,"
— Acts 20:35

THE GRACIOUS INVITATION

"Remember the words of the Lord Jesus, how He said,"

"Come unto Me, all you who labor and are heavy laden, and I will give you rest." — Matthew 11:28

Gracious "word" of a gracious Savior, on which the soul may confidingly repose, and be at peace forever! It is a present rest — the rest of grace as well as the rest of glory. Not only are there signals of peace hung out from the walls of Heaven — the lights of Home glimmering in the distance to cheer our footsteps; but we have the "shadow" of this "great Rock!" in a present "weary land." Before the Throne above is there "the sea of glass," without one rippling wave; but there is a haven even on earth for the tempest-tossed, "We who have believed DO enter into rest."

Reader, have you found this blessed repose in the blood and work of Immanuel? Long going about "seeking rest and finding none," does this "word" sound like music in your ears — "Come unto Me"? All other peace is counterfeit, shadowy, unreal. The eagle spurns the gilded cage as a poor exchange for his free-born soarings. The soul's immortal aspirations cannot be satisfied, short of the possession of God's favor and love in Jesus.

How complete is the invitation! If there had been one condition in entering this covenant Ark, we must have been through eternity at the mercy of the storm! But all are alike warranted and welcome, and none more warranted than welcome. For the weak, the weary, the sin-burdened and sorrow-burdened, there is an open door of grace.

Return, then, unto your rest, O my soul! Let the sweet cadence of this "word of Jesus" move quietly upon you amid the disquietudes of earth. Sheltered in Him, you are safe for time — safe for eternity! There may be, and will be, temporary tossings, fears, and misgivings; manifestations of inward corruption; but these will only be like the surface-heavings of the ocean, while underneath there is a deep, settled calm. "You will keep him in perfect peace" (lit. peace, peace) "whose mind is stayed on You." In the world — it is care on care, trouble on trouble, sin on sin — but every wave that breaks on the believer's soul seems sweetly to murmur, "Peace, peace!"

And if the foretaste of this rest is precious, what must be the glorious consummation? Awaking in the morning of immortality, with the unquiet dream of earth over — faith lost in sight, and hope in fruition — no more any bias to sin — no more latent principles of evil — nothing to disturb the spirit's deep, everlasting tranquility — the trembling magnet of the heart reposing, where alone it can confidingly and permanently rest — in the enjoyment of the Infinite God. "These things have I spoken unto you, that in Me you might have peace."

THE COMFORTING ASSURANCE

Acts 20:35, "Remember the words of the Lord Jesus, how He said,"

"Your heavenly Father knows that you have need of all these things." — Matthew 6:32

Though spoken originally by Jesus regarding temporal things, this may be taken as a motto for the child of God amid all the changing vicissitudes of his changing history. How it should lull all misgivings; silence all murmurings; lead to lowly, unquestioning submissiveness, "My Heavenly Father knows that I have need of all these things!"

Where can a child be safer or better — than in a father's hand? Where can the believer be better — than in the hands of his God? We are poor judges of what is best for us. We are under safe guidance with infallible wisdom. If we are tempted in a moment of rash presumption to say, "All these things are against me!" let this "word" rebuke the hasty and unworthy surmise. Unerring wisdom and Fatherly love, have pronounced all to be "needful."

My soul, is there anything that is disturbing your peace? Are providences dark, or crosses heavy? Are spiritual props removed, creature comforts curtailed, gourds smitten and withered like grass? Write on each, "Your Father knows that you have need of all these things!" It was He who increased your burden. Why? "It was needed." It was He who crossed your worldly schemes, marred your cherished hopes. Why? "It was needed." A pleasant flower in the coveted path — it was supplanting Himself — He had to remove it! There was some higher spiritual blessing in communion with God.

Seek to cherish a spirit of more childlike confidence in your Heavenly Father's will. You are not left unfriended and alone to buffet the storms of the wilderness. Your Marahs as well as your Elims are appointed by Him. A gracious pillar-cloud is before you. Follow it through sunshine and storm. He may "lead you about," but He will not lead you wrong. Unutterable tenderness is the characteristic of all His dealings. "Blessed be His name," says a tried believer, "He makes my feet like hinds' feet" (literally, "equals" them), "He equals them for every precipice, every ascent, every leap."

And who is it that speaks this quieting word? It is He who Himself felt the preciousness of the assurance during His own awful sufferings, that all were needed, and all appointed; that from Bethlehem's cradle to Calvary's Cross — there was not an unnecessary thorn in the crown of sorrow which He, the Man of Sorrows, bore. Every drop in His bitter cup was mingled by His Father: "This cup which You give Me to drink, shall I not drink it?" Oh, if He could extract comfort in this hour of inconceivable agony, in the thought that a Father's hand lighted the fearful furnace-fires — what strong consolation is there is the same truth to all His suffering people!

What! one superfluous drop! one unessential pang! one unneeded cross! Hush the secret atheism! He gave His Son for you! He calls Himself "your Father!" Whatever be the trial under which you are now smarting, let the word of a gracious Savior be "like oil thrown on the fretful sea;" let it dry every rebellious tear-drop. "He, your unerring Parent, knows that you have need of this as well as all these things."

THE POWER OF PRAYER

"Remember the words of the Lord Jesus, how He said,"

"Whatever you shall ask in my name, that will I do — that the Father may be glorified in the Son." — John 14:13

Blessed Jesus! it is You who has unlocked to Your people the gates of prayer. Without You, they must have been shut forever. It was Your atoning merit on earth that first opened them; it is Your intercessory work in Heaven that keeps them open still.

How unlimited the promise — "Whatever you shall ask!" It is the pledge of all that the needy sinner requires — all that an Omnipotent Savior can bestow! As the great Steward of the mysteries of grace, He seems to say to His faithful servants, "Take your request, and under this, My superscription, write what you please." And then, when the blank is filled up, He further endorses each petition with the words, "I WILL do it!"

He further encourages us to ask "in His name." In the case of an earthly petitioner there are some pleas more influential in obtaining a benefit than others. Jesus speaks of this as forming the key to the heart of God. As David loved the helpless cripple of Saul's house "for Jonathan's sake," so will the Father, by virtue of our covenant relationship to the true Jonathan (lit., "the gift of God"), delight in giving us even "exceedingly abundantly above all that we can ask or think."

Reader, do you know the blessedness of confiding your every need and every care — your every sorrow and every cross — into the ear of the Savior? He is the "Wonderful Counselor." With an exquisitely tender sympathy, He can enter into the innermost depths of your need. That need may be great — but the everlasting arms are underneath it all. Think of Him now, at this moment — the great Angel of the Covenant, with the censer full of much incense, in which are placed your feeblest aspirations, your most burdened sighs — the odor-breathing cloud ascending with acceptance before the Father's throne. The answer may tarry — these your supplications may seem to be kept long on the wing, hovering around the mercy-seat. A gracious God sometimes sees it fitting thus to test the faith and patience of His people. He delights to hear the music of their importunate pleadings — to see them undeterred by difficulties — unrepelled by apparent forgetfulness and neglect. But He will come at last — the pent-up fountain of love and mercy will at length burst out — the soothing accents will in His own good time be heard, "Be it unto you according to your word!"

Soldier of Christ! with all your other armor, do not forget the weapon, "All-prayer." It is that which keeps bright and shining "the whole armor of God." While yet out in the night of a dark world — while still camping in an enemy's country — kindle your watch-fires at the altar of incense. You must be Moses — pleading on the Mount; if you would be Joshua — victorious in the world's daily battle. Confide your cause to this waiting Redeemer. You cannot weary Him with your importunity. He delights in hearing. He is glorified in giving. The memorable Bethany-utterance remains unaltered and unrepealed, "I know that You hear Me always." He is still the "Prince that has power with God and prevails" — He still promises and pleads — he still He lives and loves!

THE UNVEILED DEALINGS

"Remember the words of the Lord Jesus, how He said,"

"You do not realize now what I am doing — but later you will understand."
— John 13:7

O blessed day, when the long sealed book of mystery shall be unfolded, when the "fountains of the great deep shall be broken up," "the channels of the waters seen," and all discovered to be one vast revelation of unerring wisdom and ineffable love! Here we are often baffled at the Lord's dispensations; we cannot fathom His ways — like the well of Sychar — they are deep, and we have nothing to draw with. But soon the "mystery of God will be finished;" the enigmatical "seals," with all their inner meanings, opened. When that "morning without clouds" shall break, each soul will be like the angel standing in the sun — there will be no shadow; all will be perfect day!

Believer, be still! The dealings of your Heavenly Father may seem dark to you; there may seem now to be no golden fringe, no "bright light in the clouds;" but a day of disclosures is at hand. "Take it on trust a little while." An earthly child takes on trust what his father tells him: when he reaches maturity, much that was baffling to his infant comprehension is then explained. You are in this world in the childhood of your being — Eternity is the soul's immortal manhood. There, every dealing will be vindicated. It will lose all its "darkness" when bathed in floods "of the excellent glory!"

Ah! instead of thus being as weaned children, how apt are we to exercise ourselves in matters too high for us! not content with knowing that our Father wills it — but presumptuously seeking to know how it is, and why it is. If it is unfair to pronounce on the unfinished and incomplete works of man; if the painter, or sculptor, or artificer, would shrink from having his labors judged of when in a rough, unpolished, immature state — how much more so with the works of God! How we should honor Him by a simple, confiding, unreserved submission to His will — contented patiently to wait the fulfillment of this "later" promise, when all the lights and shadows in the now half-finished picture will be blended and melted into one harmonious whole — when all the now disjointed stones in the temple will be seen to fit into their appointed place — giving unity, and symmetry, and compactness to all the building.

And who is it that speaks these living "words," "What I am doing?" It is He who died for us! who now lives for us! Blessed Jesus! You may do much that our blind hearts would like undone — "terrible things in righteousness which we looked not for." The heaviest (what we may be tempted to call the severest) cross You can lay upon us we shall regard as only the apparent severity of unutterable and unalterable love. Eternity will unfold how all — all was needed; that nothing else, nothing less, could have done! If not now, at least then — the verdict on a calm retrospect of life will be this, "The Word of the Lord is right, and all His works are done in truth."

THE FATHER GLORIFIED

"Remember the words of the Lord Jesus, how He said,"

"Herein is My Father glorified — that you bear much fruit; showing yourselves to be My disciples." — John 15:8

When surveying the boundless ocean of covenant mercy — every wave chiming, "God is Love!" — does the thought ever present itself, "What can I do for this great Being who has done so much for me?" Recompense, I cannot! No more can my purest services add one iota to His un-derived glory, than the tiny candle can add to the blaze of the sun at noonday, or a drop of water to the boundless ocean. Yet, wondrous thought! from this worthless soul of mine there may roll in a revenue of glory which He who loves the broken and contrite spirit will "not despise." "Herein is My Father glorified — that you bear much fruit."

Reader! are you a fruit-bearer in your Lord's vineyard? Are you seeking to make life one grand act of consecration to His glory — one thank-offering for His unmerited love? You may be unable to exhibit much fruit in the eye of the world. Your circumstances and position in life may forbid you to point to any splendid services, or laborious and imposing efforts in the cause of God. It matters not. It is often those fruits that are unseen and unknown to man, ripening in seclusion — that He values most — the quiet, lowly walk — patience and submission — gentleness and humility — putting yourself unreservedly in His hands — willing to be led by Him even in darkness — saying, Not my will — but Your will — the unselfish spirit, the meek bearing of an injury, the unostentatious kindness; these are some of the "fruits" which your Heavenly Father loves, and by which He is glorified.

Perchance it may be with you the season of trial, the chamber of protracted sickness, the time of desolating bereavement, some furnace seven times heated. Herein, too, you may sweetly glorify your God. Never is your Heavenly Father more glorified by His children on earth, than when, in the midst of these furnace-fires, He listens to nothing but the gentle breathings of confiding faith and love, "Let Him do what seems good unto Him." Yes — you can, there in the furnace, glorify Him in a way which angels cannot do in a world where they have no trials. They can glorify God only with the crown; you can glorify Him with the cross and the prospect of the crown together! Ah, if He is dealing severely with you — if He, as the Great Gardener, is pruning His vines, lopping their boughs, and stripping off their luxuriant branches — remember the end! "He prunes it — that it may bring forth more fruit," and "Herein is My Father glorified!"

Be it yours to lie passive in His hands, saying in unmurmuring resignation, "Father, glorify Your name! Glorify Yourself, whether by giving — or taking, filling my cup — or "emptying me from vessel to vessel! Let me know no will but Yours!" Angels possess no higher honor and privilege than glorifying the God before whom they cast their crowns. How blessed to be able thus to claim brotherhood with the spirits in the upper sanctuary! No, more, to be associated with the Savior Himself in the theme of His own exalted joy, when He said, "I have glorified You on earth!" "These things have I spoken unto you, that My joy might remain in you, and that your joy might be full."

THE TENDER SOLICITUDE

"Remember the words of the Lord Jesus, how He said,"

"The very hairs of your head are all numbered!" — Matthew 10:30

What a "word" is this! All that befalls you, to the very numbering of your hairs — is known to God! Nothing can happen by accident or chance. Nothing can elude His inspection. The fall of the forest leaf — the fluttering of the insect — the waving of the angel's wing — the annihilation of a world — all are equally noted by Him! Man speaks of great things and small things — but God knows no such distinction.

How especially comforting to think of this tender solicitude with reference to His own covenant people — that He metes out all their joys — and all their sorrows! Every sweet--and every bitter--is ordained by Him. Even "wearisome nights" are "appointed." Not a pang I feel, not a tear I shed — but is known to Him. What are called "dark dealings," are the ordinations of undeviating faithfulness. Man may err — his ways are often crooked; "but as for God — His way is perfect!" He puts my tears into His bottle. Every moment His everlasting arms are underneath and around me. He keeps me "as the apple of His eye." He "bears" me as a man bears his own son!

Do I look to the FUTURE? Is there much of uncertainty and mystery hanging over it? It may be, much foreboding of evil. Trust Him. All is marked out for me. Dangers will be averted; bewildering mazes will show themselves to be interlaced and interweaved with mercy. "He keeps the feet of His saints." Not a hair of their head will be touched.

He leads sometimes darkly, sometimes sorrowfully; most frequently by cross and circuitous ways, which we ourselves would not have chosen; but always wisely, always tenderly. With all its mazy windings and turnings, its roughness and ruggedness — the believer's is not only a right way — but the right way — the best which covenant love and wisdom could select.

"Nothing," says Jeremy Taylor, "does so establish the mind amid the rollings and turbulence of present things — as both a look above them and a look beyond them; above them — to the steady and loving hand by which they are ruled; and beyond them — to the sweet and beautiful end to which, by that hand, they will be brought." "The Great Counselor," says Thomas Brooks, "puts clouds and darkness round about Him, bidding us follow at His beck through the cloud, promising an eternal and uninterrupted sunshine on the other side." On that "other side" we shall see how every apparent rough blast has been hastening our boats nearer the desired haven.

Well may I commit the keeping of my soul to Jesus in well-doing — as unto a faithful Creator. He gave Himself for me. This transcendent pledge of love — is the guarantee for the bestowment of every other needed blessing. Oh, blessed thought! my sorrows are numbered--by the Man of Sorrows; my tears are counted--by Him who shed first His tears, and then His blood for me! He will impose no needless burden, and exact no unnecessary sacrifice. There was no unnecessary drop in the cup of His own sufferings; neither will there be in that of His people. "Though He slays me — yet will I trust in Him!" "Therefore comfort one another with these words."

THE GOOD SHEPHERD

"Remember the words of the Lord Jesus, how He said,"

"I am the Good Shepherd. I know My sheep — and My sheep know Me."
— John 10:14

"The Good Shepherd" — well can the sheep who know His voice, attest the truthfulness and faithfulness of this endearing name and word. Where would they have been through eternity — had He not left His throne of light and glory, traveling down to this dark valley of the curse, and giving His life a ransom for them? Think of His love to each separate member of the flock — wandering over pathless wilds with unwearied patience and unquenchable ardor, ceasing not the pursuit — until He finds it.

Think of His love now — "I AM the Good Shepherd." Still that tender eye of watchfulness following the guilty wanderers — the glories of Heaven and the songs of angels unable to dim or alter His affection — the music of the words, at this moment coming as sweetly from His lips as when first He uttered them, "I know My sheep." Every individual believer — the weakest, the weariest, the faintest — claims His attention. His loving eye follows me day by day out to the wilderness — marks out my pasture, studies my needs, and trials, and sorrows, and perplexities — every steep ascent, every brook, every winding path, every thorny thicket!

"He goes before them." It is not rough driving — but gentle guiding. He does not take them over an unknown road; He Himself has trodden it before. He has drunk of every "brook by the way;" He Himself has "suffered being tempted;" He is "able to support those who are tempted." He seems to say, "Fear not! I cannot lead you wrong; follow Me in the bleak wasteland, the blackened wilderness — as well as by the green pastures and the still waters. Do you ask why I have left the sunny side of the valley — carpeted with flowers, and bathed in sunshine — leading you to some high mountain alone, some cheerless spot of sorrow? Trust Me! I will lead you by paths you have not known — but they are all known to Me, and selected by Me — Follow Me!"

"My sheep know Me!" Reader! can you subscribe to these closing words of this gracious utterance? Do you "know" Him in all the glories of His person — in all the completeness of His finished work — in all the tenderness and unutterable love of His every dealing towards you?

It has been remarked by Palestine travelers, that not only do the sheep there follow the guiding shepherd — but even while eating the herbage as they go along, they look wistfully up to see that they are near him. Is this your attitude — "looking unto Jesus?" "In all your ways acknowledge Him — and He will direct your paths." Leave the future — to His providing. "The Lord is my Shepherd — I shall not lack." I shall not lack! — it has been beautifully called "the bleating of Messiah's sheep." Take it as your watchword during your wilderness wanderings, until grace is perfected in glory. Let this be the record of your simple faith and unwavering trust, "These are those who follow — wherever He sees fit to guide them." "His sheep follow Him — for they know His voice."

THE ABIDING COMFORTER

"Remember the words of the Lord Jesus, how He said,"

"And I will ask the Father, and He shall give you another Comforter, that He may abide with you forever." — John 14:16

When one beloved earthly friend is taken away — how the heart is drawn out towards those that remain! Jesus was now about to leave His sorrowing disciples. He directs them to one whose presence would fill up the vast blank which His own absence was to make. His name was, The Comforter; His mission was, "to abide with them forever." Accordingly, no sooner had the gates of Heaven closed on their ascended Lord, than, in fulfillment of His own gracious promise, the bereaved and orphaned Church was baptized with Pentecostal fire. "When I depart — I will send Him to you."

Reader, do you realize your privilege — living under the dispensation of the Spirit? Is it your daily prayer that He may come down in all the plenitude of His heavenly graces on your soul, even "as rain upon the mown grass, and showers that water the earth?" You cannot live without Him; there cannot be one heavenly aspiration, not one breathing of love, not one upward glance of faith — without His gracious influences! Apart from Him — there is no preciousness in the Word, no blessing in ordinances, no permanent sanctifying results in affliction. As the angel directed Hagar to the hidden spring — so this blessed Agent, true to His name and office, directs His people to the waters of comfort, giving new glory to the promises, investing the Savior's character and work with new loveliness and beauty.

How precious is the title which this "Word of Jesus" gives Him — the COMFORTER! What a word for a sorrowing world! The Church militant has its tent pitched in a "valley of tears." The name of the divine visitor, who comes to her and ministers to her needs, is — the Comforter. Wide is the family of the afflicted — but He has a healing balm for all — the weak, the tempted, the sick, the sorrowing, the bereaved, the dying! How different from other "sons of consolation!" Human friends — a look may alienate; adversity may estrange; death must separate! The "Word of Jesus" speaks of One whose attribute and prerogative is to "abide with us forever" — superior to all vicissitudes — surviving death itself!

And surely if anything else can endear His mission of love to His Church, it is that He comes direct from God, as the fruit and gift of Jesus' intercession, "I will ask the Father." This Holy Dove of peace and comfort is let out by the hand of Jesus — from the ark of covenant mercy within the veil! Nor is the gift more glorious — than it is free. Does the word, the look, of a suffering child — get the eye and the heart of an earthly father? "If you, then being evil, know how to give good gifts unto your children — how much more shall your Father in Heaven give the Holy Spirit unto those who ask Him?" It is He who makes these "words of Jesus" "winged words." "He shall bring all things to your remembrance, whatever I have said to you."

THE GRACIOUS VERDICT

"Remember the words of the Lord Jesus, how He said,"

"Neither do I condemn you; go, and sin no more!" — John 8:11

How much more tender is Jesus — than the tenderest of earthly friends! The

Apostles, in a moment of irritation, would have called down fire from heaven on obstinate sinners — but their Master rebuked the unkind suggestion.

Peter, the trusted but treacherous disciple, expected nothing but harsh and merited reproof for faithlessness — but He who knew well how that heart would be bowed with penitential sorrow, sends first the kindest of messages, and then the gentlest of rebukes — "Do you love Me?"

The watchmen in the Song of Solomon smote the bride, tore off her veil, and loaded her with reproaches — but when she found her lost Lord, there was not one word of upbraiding from Him! "So slow is He to anger," says an illustrious believer, "so ready to forgive, that when His prophets lost all patience with the people so as to make intercession against them — yet even then, He could not cast off His people whom He foreknew, for His great Name's sake."

The guilty sinner to whom He speaks this comforting "word" above, was frowned upon by her accusers. But, if others spurned her from their presence, "Neither do I condemn you," Well it is to fall into the hands of this blessed Savior-God, for great are His mercies!

Are we to infer from this, that He merely winks at sin? Far from it! His blood, His work — Bethlehem, and Calvary, refute the thought! Before the guilt even of one solitary soul could be washed out — He had to descend from His everlasting throne to agonize on the accursed tree. But this "word of Jesus" is a word of tender encouragement to every sincere, broken-hearted penitent — that crimson sins, and scarlet sins — are no barrier to a free, full, everlasting forgiveness.

The Israelite of old, gasping in his agony in the sands of the wilderness, had but to "look — and live!" And still does He say, "Look unto Me — and be saved, all the ends of the earth!" Upreared by the side of His own cross there was a monumental column for all time, only second to itself in wonder. Over the head of the dying felon is the superscription written for despairing guilt and trembling penitence, "This is a faithful saying, and worthy of all acceptance, that Jesus Christ came into the world to save sinners." "He never yet," says Charnock, "put out a dim candle that was lighted at the Sun of Righteousness." "Whatever our guiltiness is," says Rutherford, "yet when it falls into the sea of God's mercy, it is but like a drop of blood fallen into the great ocean!"

Reader, you may be the chief of sinners — or it may be the chief of backsliders; your soul may have veered astray like an arrow from a broken bow. As the bankrupt is afraid to look into his books — so you may be afraid to look into your own heart! You are hovering on the verge of despair. Conscience, and the memory of unnumbered sins, is uttering the desponding verdict, "I condemn you!" Jesus has a kinder word — a more cheering declaration, "Neither do I condemn you; go, and sin no more!" "And all wondered at the gracious WORDS that proceeded out of His mouth!"

THE WONDROUS RELATIONSHIP

"Remember the words of the Lord Jesus, how He said,"

"For whoever shall do the will of God — the same is My brother, and My sister, and mother." — Mark 3:35

As if no solitary earthly type were enough to image forth the love of Jesus, He assembles into one verse — a group of the tenderest earthly relationships. Human affection has to focus its loveliest hues — but all is too little to adequately expatiate the depth and intensity of His love. He is "Son," "Brother," "Friend" — all in one; "cleaving closer than any brother."

And can we wonder at such language? He gave Himself for us; after that pledge of His affection — we must cease to marvel at any expression of the interest He feels in us. Anything that He can say or do for us now — is infinitely less than what He has done.

Believer! are you solitary and desolate? Has bereavement severed earthly ties? Has the grave made forced estrangements — sundered the closest links of earthly affection? In Jesus you have filial and fraternal love combined; He is the Friend of friends, whose presence and fellowship compensates for all losses, and supplies all blanks! If you are orphaned, friendless, comfortless here, remember that there is in the Elder Brother on the Throne — a love deep as the unfathomed ocean, and boundless as Eternity!

And who are those who can claim the blessedness spoken of under this wondrous imagery? On whom does He lavish this unutterable affection? No mere outward profession will purchase it. No church, no priest, no ordinances, no denominational distinctions are sufficient.

It is for those who are possessed of holy characters. "He who does the will of My Father who is in Heaven!" He who reflects the mind of Jesus; imbibes His Spirit; takes His Word as the regulator of his daily walk, and makes His glory the great end of his being; he who lives to God, and with God, and for God; the humble, lowly, Christ-like, Heaven-seeking Christian — he it is who can claim as his own this wondrous heritage of love!

If it is a worthy object of ambition to be loved by the good and the great on earth — then what must it be to have an eye of love ever beaming upon us from the eternal Throne, in comparison of which the attachment here of brother, sister, kinsman, friend — all combined — pales like the stars before the rising sun!

Though we are often ashamed to call Him "Brother," "He is not ashamed to call us brethren." He looks down on poor worms, and says, "These are My mother, and sisters, and brothers!" "I will write upon them," He says in another place, "My new name." Just as we write our name on a book to tell that it belongs to us — so Jesus would write His own name on us, the wondrous volumes of His grace — that they may be read and pondered by principalities and powers.

Have we known and believed this astonishing love of God to us? Ah, how poor has been the requital! Who cannot subscribe to these holy words: "Your love has been as a shower to us — but our return but a dew-drop, and that dew-drop is stained with sin!" "If a man loves Me, he will keep My Words; and My Father will love him, and We will come unto him, and make Our abode with him."

THE BEFRIENDED ORPHANS

"Remember the words of the Lord Jesus, how He said,"

"I will not leave you comfortless — I will come to you." — John 14:18

Does the Christian's path lie all the way through Beulah land? No, he is forewarned it is to be one of "much tribulation." He has his Marahs — as well as his Elims; his valleys of Baca — as well as his grapes of Eshcol. Often is he left un-befriended to bear the brunt of the storm — his gourds fading when most needed — his sun going down while it is yet day — his happy home and happy heart darkened in a moment with sorrows, with which a stranger (with which often a brother) cannot understand.

But there is One Brother "born for adversity" who can understand. How often has that voice broken with its silvery accents, the muffled stillness of the sick-chamber! "I will not leave you comfortless — the world may, friends may, the desolations of bereavement and death may — but I will not! You will be alone — yet not alone, for I your Savior and your God will be with you!"

Jesus seems to have an especial love and affection for His orphaned and comfortless people. A father loves his sick and sorrowing child most; of all his household, this sick one occupies most of his thoughts. Christ seems to delight to lavish His deepest sympathy on "him that has no helper." It is in the hour of sorrow, His people have found Him most precious; it is in "the wilderness" that He speaks most "comfortable unto them." He gives them "their vineyards from thence" — in the places they least expected, wells of heavenly consolation break forth at their feet. As Jonathan of old, when faint and weary, had his strength revived by the honey he found dropping in the tangled thicket — so the faint and woe-worn children of God find "honey in the forest" — everlasting consolation dropping from the tree of life, in the midst of the thorniest thickets of affliction!

Comfortless ones — be comforted! Jesus often makes you portionless here in this world — to drive you to Himself, the everlasting portion. He often dries every rill and fountain of earthly bliss — that He may lead you to say, "All my springs are in You!" "He seems intent," says one who could speak from experience, "to fill up every gap which love has been forced to make; one of His errands from Heaven was to bind up the broken-hearted." How beautifully in one amazing verse does He conjoin the depth and tenderness of His comfort — with the certainty of it, "As one whom his mother comforts — so will I comfort you, and you SHALL be comforted!"

Ah, how many would not have their wilderness-state altered, with all its trials, and gloom, and sorrow — just so that they might enjoy the unutterable sympathy and love of this Comforter of the comfortless, one ray of whose approving smile can dispel the deepest earthly gloom! As the clustering constellations shine with the most intense luster in the midnight sky — so these "words of Jesus" come out like ministering angels in the deep dark night of earthly sorrow. We may see no beauty in them when the world is sunny and bright; but He has laid them up in store for us — for the dark and cloudy day. "These things have I told you, that when the time comes, you may remember that I told you of them."

THE WORLD CONQUERED

"Remember the words of the Lord Jesus, how He said,"

"I have told you these things, so that in me you may have peace. In this world you will have trouble. But take heart! I have overcome the world!" — John 16:33

And shall I be afraid of the world, which is already conquered? The Almighty Victor, within view of His crown, turns around to His faint and weary soldiers — and bids them take courage. They are not fighting their way through untried enemies. The God-Man Mediator "knows their sorrows." "He was tempted in every way, just as we are." "Both He who sanctifies (that is, Christ), and those who are sanctified (His people), are all of one (nature)." As the great Predecessor, He heads the pilgrim band, saying, "I will show you the path of life." The way to Heaven is consecrated by His footprints! Every thorn that wounds them — has wounded Him before. Every cross they can bear — He has borne before. Every tear they shed — He has shed before. There is one respect, indeed, in which the identity fails — He was "yet without sin;" but this recoil of His holy nature from moral evil gives Him a deeper and more intense sensibility towards those who have still corruption within, responding to temptation without.

Reader! are you ready to faint under your troubles? under a seducing world? under a wandering, wayward heart? "Consider Him who endured!" Listen to your adorable Redeemer, stooping from His Throne, and saying, "I have overcome the world." He came forth unscathed from its snares. With the same heavenly weapon which He bids you to wield — three times did He repel the Tempter, saying, "It is written!"

Is it some crushing trial — or overwhelming grief? He is "acquainted with grief." He, the mighty Vine, knows the minutest fibers of sorrow in the branches; when the pruning knife touches them — it touches Him. "He has gone," says a tried sufferer, "through every class of suffering in our wilderness school." He loves to bring His people into untried and perplexing places — that they may seek out the guiding pillar, and prize its radiance. He puts them on the darkened waves, that they may follow the guiding light hung out astern from the only Ship of pure and unsullied humanity that was ever armored against the storm.

Be assured that there is disguised love in all that He does. He who knows us infinitely better than we know ourselves, often puts a thorn in our nest to drive us to the wing — that we may not be grovelers forever. "It is," says Evans, "upon the smooth ice that we slip; the rough path is safest for the feet."

The tearless and undimmed eye — is not to be coveted here on earth; that is reserved for Heaven! Who can tell what muffled and disguised "needs be" there may lurk under these worldly troubles? His true spiritual seeds are often planted deep in the soil; they have to make their way through a load of sorrow before they reach the surface; but their roots are thereby the firmer and deeper struck. Had it not been for these lowly and needed "depths," they might have rushed up as feeble saplings, and succumbed to the first cold blast. He often leads His people still, as He led them of old, to a "high mountain, alone;" but it is to a high mountain — above the world; and, better still, He who Himself has overcome the world — leads them there, and speaks comfort unto them!

THE LITTLE FLOCK

"Remember the words of the Lord Jesus, how He said,"

"Fear not, little flock; for it is your Father's good pleasure to give you the kingdom." — Luke 12:32

The music of the Shepherd's voice again! Another comforting "word," and how tender! His flock, a little flock, a feeble flock, a fearful flock — but a beloved flock — loved of the Father, enjoying His "good pleasure," and soon to be a glorified flock — safe in the fold, secure within the kingdom! How does He quiet their fears and misgivings? As they stand panting on the bleak mountainside, He points His crook upwards to the bright and shining gates of glory, and says, "It is your Father's good pleasure to give you these!" What gentle words! what a blessed consummation! Gracious Savior, Your gentleness has made me great!

That kingdom is the believer's — by irreversible and inalienable covenant-right. Says Jesus in another place, "I appoint unto you a kingdom, as My Father has appointed unto Me." It is as sure as everlasting love and almighty power can make it. Satan, the great foe of the kingdom, may be injecting foul misgivings, doubts, and fears as to your security; but he cannot divest you of your purchased immunities! He must first pluck the crown from the 'brow upon the throne', before he can weaken or impair this sure word of promise! If "it pleased the Lord" to bruise the Shepherd — then it will surely please Him to glorify the purchased flock.

Believers, think of this! "It is your Father's good pleasure." The Good Shepherd, in leading you across the intervening mountains, shows you signals and memorials of paternal grace studding all the way. He may "lead you about" in your way there. How did He lead the children of Israel of old out of Egypt — to their promised kingdom? By forty years' wilderness discipline and privations! But trust Him; do not dishonor Him with guilty doubts and fears. Do not look back on your dark, stumbling paths, nor within on your fitful and vacillating heart; but forwards to the promised heavenly kingdom!

Let the melody of the Shepherd's voice fall gently on your ear, "It is your Father's good pleasure." I have given you, He seems to say, the best proof that it is My good pleasure. In order to purchase that kingdom — I died for you! "I will be like a shepherd looking for his scattered flock. I will find My sheep and rescue them from all the places where they were scattered on that dark and cloudy day." Fear not, then, little flock! Though for a while, you are in the bleak mountain and arid wasteland, seeking your way Zionward, it may be "with torn fleeces and bleeding feet;" for, "It is not the will of your Father who is in Heaven — that one of these little ones should perish!"

THE UNLIMITED OFFER

"Remember the words of the Lord Jesus, how He said,"

"If any man thirsts — let him come unto Me, and drink." — John 7:37

This is one of the most gracious "words" which ever "proceeded out of the mouth of God!" The time that it was uttered was an impressive one; it was on "the last, the great day" of the Feast of Tabernacles, when a denser multitude than on any of the seven preceding ones were assembled together. The golden bowl, according to custom, had probably just been filled with the waters of Siloam, and was being carried up to the Temple amid the acclamations of the crowd, when the Savior of the world seized the opportunity of speaking to them some truths of momentous import. Many, doubtless, were the "words of Jesus" uttered on the previous days — but the most important is reserved for the last. What, then, is the great closing theme on which He rivets the attention of this vast auditory, and which He would have them carry away to their distant homes? It is, The freeness of His own great Salvation, "If any man thirsts — let him come unto Me, and drink."

Reader, do you discredit the reality of this gracious offer? Are your legion sins standing as a barrier between you and a Savior's offered mercy? Do you feel as if you cannot come "just as you are;" that some partial cleansing, some preparatory reformation must take place before you can venture to the living fountain? No, "If any man."

What is freer than water? — The poorest beggar may drink "without money" from the wayside pool. That is your Lord's own picture of His own glorious salvation; you are invited to come, "without one plea," in all your poverty and need, in all your weakness and unworthiness. Remember the Redeemer's saying to the woman of Samaria. She was the chief of sinners — profligate, hardened, degraded — but He made no condition, no qualification; simple believing was all that was required, "If you knew the gift of God," you would have asked, and He would have given you "living water."

But is there not, after all, one condition mentioned in this "word of Jesus?", "If any man thirsts." You may have the depressing consciousness that you experience no such ardent longings after holiness — but only of your need of the Savior. But is not this very conviction of your need — an indication of a feeble longing after Christ? If you are saying, "I have nothing to draw with, and the well is deep," then He who makes the offer of the salvation — will Himself fill your empty vessel, "He satisfies the longing soul with goodness."

"Jesus stood and cried out." It is the solitary instance recorded of Him, of whom it is said, "He shall not strive nor cry out, nor raise His voice in the streets." But it was truth of surpassing interest and magnitude He had to proclaim. It was a declaration, moreover, especially dear to Him. As it formed the theme of this ever-memorable sermon during His public ministry, so when He was sealing up the inspired record — the last utterances of His voice on earth, until that voice shall be heard again on the throne, contained the same life-giving invitation, "Let him that is thirsty come — and whoever will, let him take of the water of life freely!" Oh! as the echoes of that gracious saying — this blast of the silver trumpet — are still sounding to the ends of the world, may this be the recorded result, "As He spoke these words — many believed on Him."

THE SONFUL SERVITUDE

"Remember the words of the Lord Jesus, how He said,"

"For My yoke is easy — and My burden is light." — Matthew 11:30

Can the same be said of Satan — or sin? With regard to them — how faithfully true rather is the reverse, "My yoke is heavy, and my burden is grievous!" Christ's service is a happy service, the only happy one; and even when there is a cross to carry, or a yoke to bear — it is His own appointment. "My yoke." It is sent by no untried friend. No, He who puts it on His people, bore this very yoke Himself. "He carried our sorrows." How blessed this feeling of holy servitude to so kind a Master! not like "dumb, driven cattle," goaded on — but led, and led often most tenderly when the yoke and the burden are upon us. The great apostle rarely speaks of himself under any other title but one. That one he seems to make his boast. He had much whereof he might glory — he had been the instrument in saving thousands — he had spoken before kings — he had been in Caesar's palace and Caesar's presence — he had been caught up into the third heaven — but in all his letters this is his joyful prefix and superscription, "The servant (literally, the slave) of Jesus Christ!"

Reader! do you know this blessed servitude? Can you say with a joyful heart, "O Lord, truly I am Your servant"? He is no hard taskmaster. Would Satan try to teach you so? Let this be the refutation, "He loved me — and gave Himself for me." True, the yoke is the appointed discipline He employs in training His children for immortality. But be comforted! "It is His tender hand that puts it on — and keeps it on." He will suit the yoke — to the neck; and the neck — to the yoke. He will suit His grace to your trials. No, He will bring you even to be in love with these, when they bring along with them such gracious unfoldings of His own faithfulness and mercy!

How His people need thus to be in heaviness through manifold temptations, to keep them meek and submissive! "Jeshurun (like a bullock unaccustomed to the harness, fed and pampered in the stall) waxed fat, and kicked!" Never is there more gracious love than when God takes means to curb and subjugate, humble us, and to prove us — bringing us out from ourselves, our likings, our confidences, our prosperity — and putting us under the needed YOKE!

And who has ever repented of that joyful servitude? Among all the regrets that mingle with a dying hour, and often bedew with bitter tears a dying pillow — who ever told of regrets and repentance here?

Tried believer — has He ever failed you? Has His yoke been too grievous? Have your tears been unalleviated — your sorrows unsolaced — your temptations above that which you were able to bear? Ah! rather can you not testify, "I cast my burden upon Him — and He sustained me!" How have seeming difficulties melted away! How has the yoke lost its heaviness, and the cross its bitterness, in the thought of who you were bearing it for! There is a promised rest in the very carrying of the yoke; and a better rest remains for the weary and toil-worn when the appointed work is finished; for thus says "that same Jesus," "Take My yoke upon you, and learn of Me — and you shall find REST unto your souls!"

THE MEASURE OF LOVE

"Remember the words of the Lord Jesus, how He said,"

"As the Father has loved Me — so have I loved you." — John 15:9

This is the most amazing verse in the Bible! Who can fathom the unimagined depths of that love which dwelt in the bosom of the Father from all eternity towards His Son? — and yet, here is the Savior's own measure of His love towards His people!

There is no subject more profoundly mysterious than those mystic inter-communings between the first and second persons in the adorable Trinity before the world was. Scripture gives us only some dim and shadowy revelations regarding them — distant gleams of light, and no more. Let one suffice. "Then I was by Him, as one brought up with Him, and I was daily His delight, rejoicing always before Him."

We know that earthly affection is deepened and intensified by increased familiarity with its object. The friendship that began only yesterday is not the sacred, hallowed thing which years of growing communion have matured. If we may with reverence apply this test to the highest type of holy affection, what must have been that interchange of love which the measureless span of Eternity had fostered — a love, moreover, not fitful, transient, vacillating, subject to altered tones and estranged looks — but pure, constant, untainted, without one shadow of turning! And yet, listen to the words of Jesus, "As the Father has loved Me — so have I loved you!"

It would have been infinitely more than we had reason to expect, if He had said, "As My Father has loved angels — so have I loved you." But the love borne to no finite beings is an appropriate symbol. Long before the birth of time or of worlds — that love existed. It was together with Eternity itself. Hear how the two themes of the Savior's eternal rejoicing — the love of His Father, and His love for sinners — are grouped together, "Rejoicing always before Him, and in the habitable part of His earth!"

To complete the picture, we must take in a counterpart description of the Father's love to us, "Therefore does My Father love Me," says Jesus in another place, "because I lay down My life!" God had an all-sufficiency in His love — He needed not the wearisome love of creatures to add to His glory or happiness; but He seems to say, that so intense is His love for us — that He loves even His beloved Son more (if infinite love be capable of increase), because He laid down His life for the guilty! It is regarding the Redeemed it is said, "He shall rest in His love — He shall rejoice over them with singing."

In the assertion, "God is love," we are left truly with no mere unproved affirmation regarding the existence of some abstract quality in the divine nature. "Herein," says the apostle, "perceive we THE LOVE of God," but, as it has been remarked, ("Our translators need not have added whose love, for there is but one such specimen"), "because He laid down His life for us." No expression of love can be wondered at, after this. Ah, how miserable are our best expressions, compared with His! "Our love is but the reflection — as cold as the moon; His is as the sun." Shall we refuse to love HIM more in return, who has first loved, and SO loved us?

THE BRIEF GOSPEL

"Remember the words of the Lord Jesus, how He said,"

"Only believe!" — Mark 5:36

The briefest of the "words of Jesus," but one of the most comforting. They contain the essence and epitome of all saving truth.

Reader, is Satan assailing you with tormenting fears? Is the thought of your sins — the guilty past — coming up in terrible memorial before you, almost tempting you to give way to hopeless despondency? Fear not! A gentle voice whispers in your ear, "Only believe. Your sins are great — but My grace and merits are greater! 'Only believe' that I died for you — that I am living for you and pleading for you, and that 'the faithful saying' is as 'faithful' as ever, and as 'worthy of all acceptance' as ever."

Are you a backslider? Did you once run well? Has your own guilty backsliding alienated and estranged you from that face which was once all love, and that service which was once all delight? Are you breathing in broken-hearted sorrow over the holy memories of a close walk with God, "Oh that it were with me as in months past, when the candle of the Lord shone on me!" "Only believe." Take this your mournful soliloquy, and convert it into a prayer. "Only believe" Him whose ways are not as man's ways, "Return O backsliding children — and I will heal your backsliding!"

Are you beaten down with some heavy trial? Have your fondest schemes been blown upon — your fairest blossoms been withered in the bud? Has wave after wave of trouble been rolling upon you? Has the Lord forgotten to be gracious? Hear the "word of Jesus" resounding amid the thickest midnight of gloom — penetrating even through the vaults of the dead, "Believe, only believe." There is an infinite reason for the trial — some lurking thorn that required removal — or some gracious lesson that required teaching. The dreadful severing blow — was dealt in love! God will be glorified in it, and your own soul made the better for it. Patiently wait until the light of immortality is reflected on a receding world. Here you must take His dealings on trust. The word of Jesus to you now is, "Only believe." The word of Jesus in eternity (every inner meaning and purpose being unfolded), "Did I not tell you — that you will see God's glory if you believe?"

Are you fearful and agitated in the prospect of death? Through fear of the last enemy, have you been all your lifetime subject to bondage? "Only believe." "As your day is — so shall your strength be." Dying grace will be given — when a dying hour comes! In the dark river, a sustaining arm will be underneath you — deeper than the deepest and darkest wave. Before you know it, the darkness will be past, the true Light shining — the whisper of faith in the nether valley. "Believe! Believe!" will be exchanged for angel-voices exclaiming, as you enter the portals of glory, "No longer through a glass darkly — but now face to face!"

Yes! Jesus Himself had no higher remedy for sin, for sorrow, and for suffering — than those two words convey. At the utmost extremity of His own distress, and of His disciples' wretchedness, He could only say "Let not your heart be troubled: you believe in God, believe also in Me." Believe — only believe. "Lord, I believe — help my unbelief."

THE GREAT CALM

"Remember the words of the Lord Jesus, how He said,"

"Take courage! It is I--do not be afraid!" — Mark 6:50

Jesus lives! His people may dispel their misgivings--for Omnipotence treads the waves! To sense it may seem at times to be otherwise--wayward accident and chance may appear to regulate human allotments; but not so!

"The Lord's voice is upon the waters!" He sits at the helm guiding the tempest-tossed bark, and guiding it well.

How often does He come to us as He did to the disciples in that midnight hour when all seems lost, "in the fourth watch of the night," — when we least looked for Him; or when, like the shipwrecked apostle, "When neither sun nor stars appeared for many days and the storm continued raging, we finally gave up all hope of being saved!" — how often just at that moment, is the "word of Jesus" heard floating over the billows, "Take courage! It is I--do not be afraid!"

Believer, are you in trouble? Listen to the voice in the storm, "It is I--do not be afraid!" That voice, like Joseph's of old to his brethren, may seem rough — but there are gracious undertones of love. "It is I!" He seems to say: "It was I — who roused the storm! It is I — who when it has done its work, will calm it, and say, 'Peace, be still.' Every wave rolls at My bidding — every trial is My appointment — all have some gracious end; they are not sent to dash you against the sunken rocks — but to waft you nearer to Heaven!"

Is it sickness? "I am He who ordained your sicknesses; the weary wasted frame, and the nights of languishing — were sent by Me!"

Is it bereavement? "I am 'the Brother' born for adversity! Your loved and lost were plucked away by Me!"

Is it death? "I am the 'Abolisher of death,' seated by your side to calm the waves of ebbing life! It is I — about to fetch My pilgrim home. It is My voice that speaks: the Master has come — and calls for you!"

Reader, you will have reason yet to praise your God for every such storm! This is the history of every heavenly voyager, "SO He brings them to their desired haven." "So!" That word, in all its unknown and diversified meaning, is in His hand. He suits His dealings to every case. "So!" With some it is through quiet seas unfretted by one buffeting wave. "So!" With others it is "mounting up to heaven, and going down again to the deep!" But whatever is the leading and the discipline, here is the grand consummation, "SO He brings them to their desired haven!" It might have been with you the moanings of an eternal night-blast — no lull or pause in the storm. But soon the darkness will be past — and the hues of morn tipping the shores of glory!

And what, then, should your attitude be? "Looking unto Jesus!" Looking away from self, and sin, and human props, and earthly refuges and confidences — and fixing the eye of unwavering and unflinching faith on a reigning Savior! Ah, how a real quickening sight of Christ — dispels all guilty fears! The Roman keepers of old were frightened, and became as dead men. The lowly Jewish women were not afraid; why? "I know that you seek Jesus!" Reader, let your weary spirit fold itself to rest under the composing "word" of a gracious Savior, saying, "I wait for the Lord, my soul does wait, and in His Word do I hope."

THE DYING LEGACY

"Remember the words of the Lord Jesus, how He said,"

"Peace I leave with you, My peace I give unto you: not as the world gives, give I unto you. Let not your heart be troubled, neither let it be afraid." — John 14:27

How we treasure the last sayings of a dying parent! How specially cherished and memorable are his last looks and last words! Here are the last words, the parting legacy, of a dying Savior. It is a legacy of peace.

What peace is this? It is His own purchase — a peace arising out of free forgiveness through His precious blood. It is sung in concert with "Glory to God in the highest" — a peace made as sure to us, as eternal power and infinite love can make it! It is peace the soul needs, that is nowhere else to be found — but through the blood of His cross! "Being justified by faith — we have peace with God." "HE gives His beloved rest!"

How different from the false and counterfeit peace in which so many are content to live, and content to die! The world's peace is all well — so long as prosperity lasts — so long as the stream runs smooth, and the sky is clear; but when the flood is at hand, or the storm is gathering, where is it? It is gone! There is no depending on its permanency. Often when the cup is fullest — there is the trembling apprehension that in one brief moment it may be dashed to the ground. The soul may be saying to itself, "Peace, peace;" but, like the writing on the sand, it may be obliterated by the first wave of adversity!

But, the peace which Jesus gives, is "not as the world gives." The peace of the believer is deep — calm — lasting — everlasting. The world, with all its blandishments, cannot give it. The world, with all its vicissitudes and fluctuations, cannot take it away! This peace is brightest — in the hour of trial; it lights up the final valley-gloom. "Mark the perfect man, and behold the upright — for the end of that man is peace!" Yes! how often is the believer's deathbed like the deep calm repose of a summer-evening's sky, when all nature is hushed to rest; the departing soul, like the vanishing sun, peacefully disappearing — only to shine in another and brighter universe! "I seem," said a Christian on his deathbed, "to have nothing to do but to wait: there is now nothing but peace, the sweetest peace."

Believer! do you know this peace which passes understanding? Is it "keeping (literally, 'garrisoning as in a citadel') your heart?" Have you learned the blessedness of waking up, morning after morning, and feeling "I am at peace with my God!" Do you know the blessedness of beholding by faith the true Aaron — the great High Priest — coming forth from "the holiest of all" to "bless His people with peace?"

Waves of trouble may be murmuring around you — but they cannot touch you! You are in the rock-crevice against which the fiercest tornado sweeps on by. Oh! leave not the making of your peace with God to a dying hour! It will be a hard thing to smooth the death-pillow, if peace with God is left unsought until then. Make sure of it now. He, the true Melchizedek, is willing now to come forth to meet you with bread and wine — emblems of peaceful gospel blessings. All the "words of Jesus" are so many streams contributing to make your peace flow as a river, "These things have I spoken unto you, that in Me you might have peace." "I will hear what God the Lord will speak, for He will speak peace unto His people and to His saints."

THE SUPREME INVESTITURE

"Remember the words of the Lord Jesus, how He said,"

"All power in heaven and in earth is given unto Me!" — Matthew 28:18

What an empire is this! Heaven and earth — the Church militant — the Church triumphant — angels and archangels — saints and seraphs are under Christ's supreme authority! At His mandate: the billows were hushed — demons crouched in terror — the grave yielded its prey! "Upon His head are many crowns!" He is made "Head over all things!" Yes! over all things, from the minutest — to the mightiest. He holds the stars in His right hand — He walks in the midst of the seven golden candlesticks, feeding every candlestick with the oil of His grace, and preserving every star in its spiritual orbit.

The Prince of Darkness has "a power," but it is not an "all power." Satan is potent — but not omnipotent. Christ holds him on a chain! He has set bounds that he may not pass over. "Satan," we read in the book of Job, "went out (with permission) from the presence of the Lord." Satan "desired" to have Peter that he might "sift him;" but there was a mightier agency at hand: "I have prayed for you," Jesus said to Peter, "that your faith will not fail!"

Believer, how often is there nothing but this grace of Jesus, between you and everlasting destruction! Satan's key may be fitting the lock in your wayward heart — but a stronger than the strong man is barring him out! The power of the adversary fanning the flame — the Omnipotence of Jesus quenching it!

Are you even now feeling the strength of your corruptions, the weakness of your graces, the presence of some outward or inward temptation? Look up to Him who has promised to make His grace sufficient for you; "all-sufficiency in all things" is His promise.

It is power, too — in conjunction with tenderness. He who sways the scepter of His universal empire "gently leads" His weak, and weary, and burdened ones! He who counts the number of the stars — loves to count the number of their sorrows! Nothing is too great — and nothing is too insignificant for Him! He paves His people's pathway, with love!

Blessed Jesus! my everlasting interests cannot be in better or in safer keeping, than in Yours. I can rely on the all-power of Your Godhead. I can sweetly rejoice in the all-sympathy of Your Manhood. I can confidently repose in the all-wisdom of Your dealings!

"Sometimes," says one, "we expect the blessing in our own way — but He chooses to bestow it in His way." But His way and His will must be the best! Infinite love, infinite power, infinite wisdom — are surely infallible guarantees! Nothing can alter His purposes. His promises can never fail. His Word never falls to the ground. "Heaven and earth shall pass away — but MY WORDS shall not pass away!"

THE DIVINE GLORIFIER

"Remember the words of the Lord Jesus, how He said,"

"He will glorify Me, because He will take from what is Mine and declare it to you." — John 16:14

The Holy Spirit glorifies Jesus in the unfoldings of His person, and His character, and His work — to His redeemed people! The Spirit is the great ministering agent between the Church on earth — and its glorified Head in Heaven. He carries up to Christ, the Intercessor on the throne — the ever-recurring needs and trials, the perplexities and sins — of each believer! And receiving out of His inexhaustible treasury of love — He carries down to us: comfort for our sorrows — strength for our tears — fullness for our emptiness!

And this the one sublime end and object of His gracious agency, "He shall glorify Me!" "When the Spirit of truth comes, He will guide you into all the truth. For He will not speak on His own, but He will speak whatever He hears." My words of sympathy — My omnipotent pleadings — the tender messages sent from an unchanged Human Heart — all these shall He speak. "He shall tell you," says Goodwin, commenting on this passage, "He shall tell you nothing but stories of My love!" He will have an ineffable delight in magnifying Me in the affections of My people, and endearing Me to their hearts! He is worthy of credence, for He is "the Spirit of truth."

How faithful has He been in every age to this, His great office as "the glorifier of Jesus!" See the first manifestation of His power in the Christian Church at the day of Pentecost. What was the grand truth which forms the focal point of interest in that unparalleled scene, and which brings three thousand stricken penitents to their knees? It is the Spirit's unfolding of Jesus — glorifying Him in eyes that before this, saw in Him no beauty! Hear the keynote of that sermon, preached "in demonstration of the Spirit, and with power,", "HIM has God exalted to be a Prince and a Savior, to give repentance to His people, and forgiveness of sins."

Ah! it is still the same peerless truth which the Spirit delights to unfold to the stricken sinner, and, in unfolding it — to make it mighty to the pulling down of strongholds. All these glorious inner beauties of Christ's work and character are undiscerned and indiscernible by the natural eye. "It is the Spirit who gives life." "No man can call Jesus Lord — but by the Holy Spirit." He is the great Forerunner — a mightier than the Baptist — proclaiming, "Behold the Lamb of God!"

Reader! any bright and realizing view you have had of the Savior's glory and excellency — is of the Spirit's imparting! When in some hour of sorrow you have been led to cleave with preeminent consolation to the thought of the Redeemer's exalted sympathy — His dying, ever-living love; or in the hour of death, when you feel the sustaining power of His exceeding great and precious promises; what is this — but the Holy Spirit, in fulfillment of His all-gracious office, taking of the things of Christ, and showing them unto you! Thus enabling you to magnify Him in your body, whether it be by life or death!

As your motto should ever be, "None but Christ!" and your ever-increasing aspiration, "More of Christ!" seek to bear in mind who it is that is alone qualified to impart the "excellency of this knowledge." "When the Comforter comes, the One I will send to you from the Father — the Spirit of truth who proceeds from the Father — He will testify about ME!"

THE JOYFUL TRANSFORMATION

"Remember the words of the Lord Jesus, how He said,"

"Your sorrow shall be turned into joy!" — John 16:20

Christ's people are a sorrowing people! Chastisement is their badge; "great tribulation" is their appointed discipline. When they enter the gates of glory, Christ is represented as wiping away tears from their eyes. But, weeping ones, be comforted! Your Lord's special mission to earth — the great errand He came from Heaven to fulfill, was "to bind up the brokenhearted." Your trials are meted out by a tender hand! He knows you too well — He loves you too well — to make this world tearless and sorrowless!

"There must be rain, and hail, and storm," says Rutherford, "in the saint's cloud." Were your earthly course strewed with flowers, and nothing but sunbeams played around your dwelling, it would lead you to forget your nomadic life — that you are but a pilgrim and sojourner here. The tent must at times be struck — the movable tabernacle taken down, pin by pin, to enable you to say and to feel with the spirit of a pilgrim, "I desire a better country!"

Meantime, while sorrow is your portion, think of Him who says, "I know your sorrows!" Angels cannot say so — they cannot sympathize with you, for trial is a strange word to them. But there is a mightier than they, who can. All He appoints for you, and sends to you — is in love. There is a provision and condition wrapped up in the bosom of every affliction, "if need be!" Coming from His hand, sorrows and riches are to His people equivalent terms. If tempted to murmur at their trials — they often murmur at disguised mercies. "Why do you ask me," said one, on his deathbed, "what I like? I am the Lord's patient — I cannot but like everything which He does."

And then, "your sorrow shall be turned into joy!" "The morning comes" — that bright morning when the dew-drops collected during earth's night of weeping shall sparkle in its beams; when in one blessed moment, a lifelong experience of trial will be effaced and forgotten — or remembered only by contrast — to enhance the fullness of the joys of immortality! What a revelation of gladness! The map of time disclosed, and every little streamlet of sorrow, every river will be seen to have been flowing heavenwards — every rough blast to have been sending the ship nearer the haven! In that joy, God Himself will participate. In the last "words of Jesus" to His people when they are standing by the triumphal archway of Glory, ready to enter on their thrones and crowns, He speaks of their joy as if it were all His own. "Enter into the joy of your Lord."

Reader, may this joy be yours! Sit loose to the world's joys. Have a feeling of chastened gratitude and thankfulness when you have them; but beware of resting in them, or investing them with a permanency which they cannot have. Jesus had His eye on Heaven when He added, "Your joy no man takes from you!"

THE OMNIPOTENT PRAYER

"Remember the words of the Lord Jesus, how He said,"

"Father, I will that those also, whom You have given Me — be with Me where I am; that they may behold My glory!" — John 17:24

This is not the petition of a suppliant — but the claim of a conqueror!

There was only one request He ever made, or ever can make — that was refused; it was the prayer wrung forth by the presence and power of superhuman anguish: "Father, if it is possible, let this cup pass from Me!" Had that prayer been answered, never could one consolatory "word of Jesus" have been ours. "If it is possible" — but for that gracious parenthesis, we must have been lost forever! In unmurmuring submission, the bitter cup was drained; all the dread penalties of the law were borne, the atonement completed, an all-perfect righteousness wrought out; and now, as the stipulated reward of His obedience and sufferings — the Victor claims His trophies.

What are they? Those who were given Him by the Father — the countless multitudes redeemed by His blood. These He "wills" to be with Him "where He is" — the spectators of His glory, and partakers of His crown! Wondrous word and will of a dying testator! His last prayer on earth is an importunate pleading for their glorification! His parting wish is to meet them in Heaven — as if these earthly jewels were needed to make His crown complete — their happiness the complement of His own!

Reader! learn from this, the grand element in the bliss of your future condition — it is the presence of Christ! "With ME — where I am." It matters comparatively little as to the locality of Heaven. "We shall see Him as He is!" is "the blessed hope" of the Christian. Heaven would be no Heaven without Jesus! The withdrawal of His presence would be like the blotting out of the sun from the skies; it would uncrown every seraph and unstring every harp! But, blessed thought! it is His own stipulation in His testamentary prayer — that Eternity is to be spent in union and communion with Himself, gazing on the unfathomed mysteries of His love, becoming more assimilated to His glorious image, and drinking deeper from the bottomless ocean of His own joy!

If anything can enhance the magnitude of this promised bliss, it is the concluding words of the verse, in which He grounds His plea for its bestowment: "I will — that they behold My glory;" — why? "For You loved (not them — but) ME before the foundation of the world!" It is equivalent to saying, "If You would give Me a continued proof of Your everlasting love and favor to Me — it is by loving and exalting My redeemed people! In loving them and glorifying them — You are loving and glorifying Me — so endearingly are their interests and My own bound up together!"

Believer, think of that all-prevailing Voice, at this moment pleading for you within the veil! — that omnipotent "Father, I will," securing every needed blessing! There is given, so to speak, a blank check by which He and His people may draw unlimited supplies out of the exhaustless treasury of the Father's grace and love! God Himself endorses it with the words, "Son, You are ever with Me — and all that I have is Yours." How it would reconcile us to Earth's bitterest sorrows, and hallow Earth's holiest joys — if we saw them thus hanging on the "will" of an all-wise Intercessor, who ever pleads in love, and never pleads in vain! "Be it unto me according to YOUR WORD."

THE IMMUTABLE PLEDGE

"Remember the words of the Lord Jesus, how He said,"

"Because I live — you shall live also!" — John 14:19

God sometimes selects the most stable and enduring objects in the material world, to illustrate His unchanging faithfulness and love to His Church, "As the mountains are round about Jerusalem, so does the Lord compass His people." But here, the Redeemer fetches an argument from His own everlasting nature. He stakes, so to speak, His own existence on that of His saints, "Because I live — you shall live also!"

Believer! read in this "word of Jesus" your glorious title-deed. Your Savior lives — and His life is the guarantee of your own. Our true Joseph is alive! He is our Brother. He talks kindly to us! That life of His, is all that is between us and everlasting ruin. But with Christ for our life, how inviolable our security! The great Fountain of being must first be dried up — before the streamlet can. The great Sun must first be quenched — before one glimmering disciple which He lights up with splendor can. Satan must first pluck the crown from that glorified Head — before he can touch one jewel in the crown of His people. They cannot shake one pillar — without first shaking the throne. "If we perish," says Luther, "Christ perishes with us!"

Reader! is your life now "hidden with Christ in God?" Do you know the blessedness of a vital and living union with a living, life-giving Savior? Can you say with humble and joyous confidence, amid the fitfulness of your own ever-changing frames and feelings, "Nevertheless I live — yet not I — but Christ lives in me"? "Jesus lives!" — They are the happiest words which a lost soul and a lost world can hear! Job, four thousand years ago, rejoiced in them. "I know," says he, "that I have a living Kinsman." John, in his Patmos exile, rejoiced in them. "I am He who lives" (or the Living One), was the simple but sublime utterance with which he was addressed by that same "Kinsman," when He appeared arrayed in the lusters of His glorified humanity.

"This is the record" (as if there was a whole gospel comprised in the statement), "that God has given to us eternal life, and this life is in His Son." Paul, in the 8th chapter to the Romans — that finest portraiture of Christian character and privilege ever drawn, begins with "no condemnation," and ends with "no separation." Why "no separation?" Because the life of the believer is incorporated with that of his adorable Head and Surety! The colossal Heart of redeemed humanity beats upon the throne — sending its mighty pulsations through every member of His body! So that, before the believer's spiritual life can be destroyed, Omnipotence must become feebleness, and Immutability become mutable! But, blessed Jesus, "Your word is very sure, therefore Your servant loves it." "I give unto them eternal life, and they shall never perish — neither shall any man pluck them out of My hand!"

THE ABIDING PRESENCE

"Remember the words of the Lord Jesus, how He said,"

"Surely, I am with you always — even unto the end of the world!" — Matthew 28:20

Such were "the words of Jesus" when He was just about to ascend to Heaven. The mediatorial throne was in view — the harps of glory were sounding in His ears; but all His thoughts are on the pilgrim Church He is to leave behind. His last words and benedictions are for them. "I go," He seems to say, "to Heaven, to My purchased crown — to the fellowship of angels — to the presence of My Father; but, nevertheless, surely I am with you always, even unto the end of the world."

How faithfully did the Apostles, to whom this promise was first addressed, experience its reality! Hear the testimony of the beloved disciple who had once leaned on his Divine Master's bosom — who "had heard, and seen, and looked upon Him." That glorified bosom was now hidden from his sight; but does he speak of an absent Lord, and of His fellowship only among the holy memories of the past? No! with rejoicing emphasis he can exclaim, "Truly our fellowship is with Jesus Christ!"

Amid so much that is fleeting here — how the heart clings to this assurance of the abiding presence of the Savior! Our best earthly friends — a few weeks may estrange them! But centuries have rolled on — Christ is still the same! How blessed to think that if I am indeed a child of God, there is not the lonely instant I am without His guardianship! When the beams of the morning visit my chamber — the brighter beams of a brighter Sun are shining upon me. When the shadows of evening are gathering around, "it is not night, if He, the unsetting 'Sun of my soul,' is near!"

His is no fitful companionship — present in prosperity — but gone in adversity. He never changes. He is always the same — in sickness and solitude, in joy and in sorrow, in life and in death! Not more faithfully did the pillar-cloud and column of fire of old precede Israel, until the last murmuring ripple of Jordan fell on their ears on the shores of Canaan — than does the presence and love of Jesus abide with His people! Has His word of promise ever proved false? Let the great cloud of witnesses now in glory testify. "Not one thing has failed of all that the Lord our God has spoken!" This "word of the Lord is tried!", "having loved His own, who were in the world — He loved them unto the end!"

Believer! are you troubled and tempted? Do dark providences and severe afflictions seem to belie the truth and reality of this gracious assurance? Are you ready, with Gideon, to say, "If the Lord is indeed with us — then why has all this befallen us?" Be assured He has some faithful end in view. By the removal of prized and cherished earthly props and refuges — He would unfold more of His own tenderness. Amid the wreck and ruin of earthly joys, which, it may be, the grave has hidden from your sight — One nearer, dearer, tenderer still, would have you say of Himself, "The Lord lives! Blessed be my Rock — and let the God of my salvation be exalted!" "Thanks be to God, who always makes us to triumph in Christ." Yes! and never more so than when, stripped of all competing objects of creature affection — we are left, like the disciples on the mount, with "Jesus only!" "These things have I spoken unto you, that in Me you might have peace."

THE RESURRECTION AND THE LIFE

"Remember the words of the Lord Jesus, how He said,"

"I am the resurrection, and the life! He who believes in Me, though he were dead — yet shall he live!" — John 11:25

What a voice is this breaking over a world which for six thousand years has been a dormitory of sin and death! For four thousand of these years, heathendom could observe no light through the bars of the grave; her oracles were speechless on the great doctrine of a future state, and more especially regarding the body's resurrection. Even the Jewish Church, under the Old Testament dispensation, seemed to enjoy little more than fitful and uncertain glimmerings, like men groping in the dark!

It required death's great Abolisher to show, to a benighted world — the luminous "path of life." With Him rested the "bringing in of a better hope" — the unfolding of "the mystery which had been hidden from ages and generations." Marvelous disclosure! that this mortal frame, decomposed and resolved into its original dust — shall yet rise from its ashes, remodeled and reconstructed, "a glorified body!" Not like "the earthly tabernacle" (a mere shifting and movable tent, as the word denotes) — but incorruptible — immortal! The beauteous transformation of the butterfly from its embryo state — the buried seed springing up from its tiny grave to the full-eared corn or gorgeous flower — these are nature's mute utterances as to the possibility of this great truth, which required the unfoldings of "a more sure word of prophecy."

But the Gospel has fully revealed what Reason, in her loftiest imaginings, could not have dreamt of! Jesus "has brought life and immortality to light!" He, the Bright and Morning Star, has "turned the shadow of death — into the morning!" He gives, in His own resurrection, the pledge of that of His people — He is the first-fruits of the immortal harvest yet to be gathered into the garner of Heaven!

Precious truth! This "word of Jesus" spans like a celestial rainbow the entrance to the dark valley. Death is robbed of its sting! In the case of every child of God — the grave holds in custody precious dust, because it is redeemed! Do not talk of it as being committed to an earthly tomb! It is locked up, rather, in the casket of God until the day "when He makes up His jewels," when it will be fashioned in deathless beauty like unto the glorified body of the Redeemer! Angels, meanwhile, are commissioned to keep watch over it, until the trumpet of the archangel shall proclaim the great "resurrection of creation." They are the "reapers," waiting for the world's great "Harvest Home," when Jesus Himself shall come again — not as He once did, humiliated and in sorrow — but rejoicing in the thought of bringing back all His redeemed sheaves with Him!

Afflicted and bereaved Christian! — you who may be mourning in bitterness over those who have died — rejoice through your tears, in these hopes "full of immortality." The silver cord is only "loosed," not broken. Perchance, as you stand in the chamber of death, or by the brink of the grave — in the depths of that awful solitude and silence which reigns around — this may be your plaintive and mournful soliloquy, "Shall the dust praise You?" Yes, it shall! This very dust shall through eternity praise its redeeming God — it shall proclaim His truth! "Lord, to whom shall we go but to You; You have the WORDS of ETERNAL LIFE."

THE LITTLE WHILE

"Remember the words of the Lord Jesus, how He said,"

"In a little while — you will see Me no more; and then after a little while — you will see Me!" — John 16:16

Long seem the moments when we are separated from the friend we love. An absent brother — how his return is looked and longed for! The "Elder Brother" — the "Living Kinsman" — sends a message to His waiting Church and people — a word of solace, telling that soon ("in a little while"), and He will be back again, never again to leave them!

There are indeed blessed moments of communion which the believer enjoys with His beloved Lord now; but how fitful and transient! Today, life is a brief Emmaus Journey — the soul happy in the presence and love of an unseen Savior. Tomorrow, He is gone; and the bereft spirit is led to interrogate itself in plaintive sorrow, "Where is now your God?" Even when there is no such experience of darkness and depression, how much there is in the world around to fill the believer with sadness! His Lord rejected and disowned — His love spurned — His providences slighted — His name blasphemed — His creation groaning and travailing in pain — disunion, too, among His people — His loving heart wounded in the house of His friends!

But, in just a little while — all this mystery of iniquity will be finished! The absent Brother's footfall will soon be heard — no longer "as a wayfaring man who turns aside to tarry for a night," but to receive His people into the permanent "mansions" His love has been preparing, and from which they shall never leave! Oh, blessed day! when creation will put on her resurrection robes — when her Lord, so long dishonored, will be enthroned amid the Hosannas of a rejoicing universe — angels lauding Him — saints crowning Him; and sin, the dark plague-spot on His universe, extinguished forever — death swallowed up in eternal victory!

And it is but "in a little while!" "Yet in a little while," we elsewhere read, "and He who shall come — will come, and will not tarry." "He will stay not a moment longer," says Goodwin, "than He has dispatched all our business in Heaven for us." With what joy will He send His mission-Angel with the announcement, "the little while is at an end!" and to issue the invitation to the great festival of glory, "Come! For all things are now ready!"

Child of sorrow! think often of this "little while." "The days of your mourning will soon be ended." There is a limit set to your suffering time, "After you have suffered for a while." Every wave is numbered, between you and the haven; and then when that haven is reached, oh, what an apocalypse of glory! The "little while" of time merged into the great and unending "while" of eternity! — to be forever with the Lord — the same unchanged and unchanging Savior!

"In a little while — and you shall see Me!" Would that the eye of faith might be kept more intently fixed on "that glorious appearing!" How the world, with its guilty fascinations, tries to dim and obscure this blessed hope! How the heart is prone to throw out its tendrils into the earth, and get them rooted in some perishable object! Reader! seek to dwell more habitually on this the grand consummation of all your dearest wishes! "Stand on the edge of your nest — pluming your wings for flight!"

THE BEATIFIC VISION

"Remember the words of the Lord Jesus, how He said,"

"Blessed are the pure in heart: for they shall see God!" — Matthew 5:8

Here is Heaven! This "word of Jesus" represents the future state of the glorified to consist not in locality — but in character; the essence of its bliss is the full vision and fruition of God! Our attention is called away from all vague and indefinite theories about the circumstantials of future happiness. The one grand object of contemplation — the "glory which excels," is the sight of God Himself! The one grand practical lesson enforced on His people, is the cultivation of that purity of heart without which none could see, or (even could we suppose it possible to be admitted to see Him) none could enjoy God!

Reader, have you attained any of this heart-purity and heart-preparation? It has been beautifully said that "the openings of the streets of Heaven — are on earth." Even here we may enjoy, in the possession of holiness — some foretaste of coming bliss. Who has not felt that the happiest moments of their lives, were those of close walking with God — nearness to the mercy-seat — when self was surrendered, and the eye was directed to the glory of Jesus, with most single, unwavering, undivided aim?

What will Heaven be — but the entire surrender of the soul to Him, without any bias to evil, without the fear of corruption within, echoing to temptation without; every thought brought into captivity to the obedience of Christ; no contrariety to His mind; all in blessed unison with His will! And the whole being impregnated with holiness: the intellect — purified and ennobled, consecrating all its powers to His service; the memory — a holy repository of pure and hallowed recollections; the affections — without one competing rival, purged from all the dross of earthliness; the love of God — the one supreme animating passion; the glory of God — the motive principle interfused through every thought, feeling, and action of the life immortal! In one word, the heart a clear fountain — no sediment to dim its purity, "no angel of sorrow" to come and trouble the pool! The long night of life over, and this is the glory of the eternal morrow which follows it: "I shall be satisfied — when I awake with Your likeness!"

Yes, this is Heaven, subjectively and objectively — purity of heart and "God all in all!" Much, doubtless, there may and will be of a subordinate kind, to intensify the bliss of the redeemed: communion with saints and angels; re-admission into the society of death-divided friends. But all these will fade before the great central glory: "God Himself shall be with them, and be their God! They shall see His face!"

Believers have been aptly called 'sunflowers' — turning their faces as the sunflower, towards the Sun of Righteousness; and hanging their leaves in sadness and sorrow — when that Sun is away. It will be in Heaven, that the emblem is complete. There, every flower in the heavenly garden will be turned God-wards, bathing its tints of loveliness in the all-excelling glory of God! Reader, may it be yours, to know all the marvels contained in these few glowing words, "We shall be like Him — for we shall see Him as He is!" "And every man who has this hope in Him — purifies himself, even as He is pure."

THE MANY MANSIONS

"Remember the words of the Lord Jesus, how He said,"

"In My Father's house are many mansions!" — John 14:2

What a 'home aspect' there is in this "word of Jesus!" He comforts His Church by telling those, whose wilderness wanderings will soon be finished — that the tented tabernacle suited to their present probation-state will be exchanged for an enduring "mansion!" Nor will it be a strange dwelling — but a Father's home! A Father's welcome awaits them! There will be accommodation for all God's redeemed people. Thousands have already entered — patriarchs, prophets, saints, martyrs, young and old — and still there is room!

The pilgrim's motto on earth is, "Here on earth — we have no continuing city." Even "Sabbath tents" must be taken down. Holy seasons of communion must terminate. "Arise, let us go from here!" is a summons which disturbs the sweetest moments of tranquility in the Church below. But in Heaven, every believer becomes a pillar in the temple of God, and "he shall go out no more." Here on earth, it is but the lodging of a wayfarer turning aside to tarry for the brief night. Here we are but temporary tenants — our possessions are all transient — ours today — but gone tomorrow! But these many "mansions" are an incorruptible and eternal inheritance! Nothing can touch the heavenly inheritance. Once within our Father's house — and we are in His house forever!

Think, too, of Jesus, gone to prepare these mansions, "I go to prepare a place for you." What a wondrous thought — Jesus now busied in Heaven — on His Church's behalf! He can find no abode in all His wide dominions, befitting as a permanent dwelling for His ransomed ones. He says, "I will make a new heaven and a new earth. I will establish a special kingdom — eternal mansions expressly for those I have redeemed with My blood!"

Reader, let the prospect of a dwelling in this "house of the Lord forever," reconcile you to any of the roughness or difficulties in your present path — to your pilgrim provision and pilgrim fare. Let the distant beacon light, that so cheeringly speaks of a Home, brighter and better far than the happiest of earthly ones — lead you to forget the intervening billows, or to think of them only as wafting you nearer to your desired glorious haven! "Would," says a saint, who has now entered on his rest, "that one could read, and write, and pray, and eat and drink, and compose one's self to sleep, as with the thought — soon I will be in Heaven, and that forever and ever!"

"My Father's house!" How many a departing spirit has been cheered and consoled by the sight of these glorious Mansions looming through the mists of the dark valley of death — the tears of weeping friends rebuked by the gentle chiding, "If you loved Me — you would rejoice, because I said, I go to My Father!" Death truly is but the entrance to our Father's house! We speak of the "shadow of death" — it is only the shadow which falls on the portico — as we stand for a moment knocking at the longed-for gate! Then next — a Father's voice of welcome is heard, "Son! you are always to be with Me, and all that I have is yours!"

THE PROMISED RETURN

"Remember the words of the Lord Jesus, how He said,"

"I will come again--and receive you unto Myself; that where I am--there you may be also!" — John 14:3

Another "word of promise" concerning the Church's "blessed hope." Orphaned pilgrims, dry your tears! Soon the Morning Hour will strike, and the sighs of a groaning and burdened creation will be heard no more! Earth's six thousand years of toil and sorrow are waning; the eternal Sabbath is at hand! Jesus will soon be heard to repeat concerning all His sleeping saints, what He said of old regarding one of them: "I go to awake him out of sleep!"

Your beloved Lord's first coming was in humiliation and woe; His name was, "the Man of Sorrows;" He had to travel on His blood-stained path, amid darkness and desertion; a crown of thorns was the only crown He bore!

But soon He will come "the second time without a sin-offering, unto salvation," never again to leave His Church — but to receive those who followed Him in His cross, to be everlasting partakers with Him in His glorious crown!

He may seem to tarry. The natural world, in her unvarying and undeviating sequences, gives no indication of His approach. Centuries have elapsed since He uttered the promise — and still He lingers; the everlasting hills wear no streak of approaching dawn; we seem to listen in vain for the noise of His chariot wheels. "But the Lord is not slack concerning His promise;" He gives you "this promise" in addition to many others as a keepsake — a pledge and guarantee for the certainty of His return, "I will come again!"

Who can conceive all the surpassing blessedness connected with His second coming? The Elder Brother arrived to fetch the younger brethren home! The true Joseph revealing Himself in tenderness to the brethren who were once estranged from Him, "receiving them to Himself" — not satisfied with apportioning a kingdom for them — but, as if all His own joy and bliss were intermingled with theirs, "Where I am," says He, "there you must be also." "He who overcomes, I will grant to sit with Me on My Throne!"

Believer, can you now say with some of the holy transport of the apostle, "Whom having not seen — we love"? What must it be when you come to see Him "face to face," and that forever and ever! If you can tell of precious hours of communion in a sin-stricken, woe-worn world, with a treacherous heart, and an imperfect or divided love — then what must it be when you come, in a sinless, sorrowless state, with purified and renewed affections — to see the King in His beauty!

The letter of an absent brother, as cheering and consolatory as it is — is a poor compensation for the joys of personal and visible communion with him. The absent Elder Brother on the Throne speaks to you now only by His Word and Spirit — soon you shall be admitted to His immediate fellowship, seeing Him "as He is" — He Himself unfolding the wondrous chart of His providence and grace — leading you about from fountain to fountain among the living waters, and with His own gentle hand wiping the last lingering tear-drop from your eye!

Heaven is an everlasting home with Jesus! "Where I am — there you may be also!" He has added a cheering postscript to this promise, on which He has caused us to hope: "He which testifies these things says, surely I come quickly!"

THE CLOSING BENEDICTION

"Remember the words of the Lord Jesus, how He said,"

"Blessed are those servants, whom the Lord when He comes — shall find watching!" — Luke 12:37

Child of God! is this your attitude, as the expectant of your Lord's appearing? Are your loins girded, and your lights burning? If the cry were to break upon your ears this day, "Behold the Bridegroom comes!" could you joyfully respond, "Yes, this is my God, I have waited for Him!"

WHEN He may come, we cannot tell — ages may elapse before then. It may be centuries before our graves are gilded with the beams of a Millennial sun; but while He may or may not come soon — He must come at some time — yes, and the day of our death — is virtually to all of us, the day of His coming.

Reader! do not put off the solemn preparation. Do not be deceived or deluded with the mocker's presumptuous challenge, "Where is the promise of His coming?" See to it that the enticements of an engrossing world, do not foster this procrastinating spirit. It may be now — or never with you. Do not put off your sowing time — until harvest time! Leave nothing for a dying hour — but to die, and calmly to resign your spirit into the hands of Jesus. Of all times, that is the least suitable: to attempt to get the vessel filled with oil; to attend to the great business of life — when life is ebbing; to trim the lamp — when the oil is finished, and it is flickering in its socket; to begin to watch — when the summons is heard to leave the watchtower to meet our God!

Were you ever struck how often, amid the many gentle words of Jesus, the summons "to watch" is over and over repeated — to rouse a sleeping Church and a slumbering world? Let this last "Word" of your Lord's send you to your knees with the question, "Am I indeed a servant of Christ?" Have I fled to Him, and am I reposing in Him, as my only Savior? Or am I still lingering like Lot — when I should be escaping? Am I only sleeping — when I should be waking? Am I only neglecting and trifling — when "a long eternity is lying at my door!" If I neglect Him who is my last and only refuge — then all is lost!

Believer! you who are standing on your watchtower — be more faithful than ever at your post. Remember what is implied in watching. It is no dreamy state of inactive torpor! It is a holy jealousy over the heart — wakeful vigilance regarding sin — every avenue and loophole of the soul carefully guarded! Holy living is the best, the only, preparative for holy dying! "Persuade yourself," says Rutherford, "that the King is coming. Read His letter sent before Him: Behold I come quickly!"

Let these "Words of Jesus" we have now been meditating upon in this little volume, be as the Golden Bells of old, hung on the vestments of the officiating High Priest, emitting sweet sounds to His spiritual Israel — telling that the true High Priest is still living and pleading in "the Holiest of all;" and that soon He will come forth to pour His blessing on His waiting Church.

We have been pleasingly employed in gathering up a few "crumbs" falling from "the Master's table." Soon we shall have, not the "Words" but the Presence of Jesus — not the crumbs falling from His table — but everlasting fellowship with the Master Himself! "Amen, even so, come, Lord Jesus!"

www.ingramcontent.com/pod-product-compliance
Lightning Source LLC
LaVergne TN
LVHW062358180726
843498LV00009B/1361